Joining
Materials

Chris Oxlade

WAYLAND

First published in Great Britain in 2006 by Wayland,
an imprint of Hachette Children's Books

Copyright © 2006 Wayland

Hachette Children's Books
338 Euston Road, London NW1 3BH

Editor: Hayley Leach
Senior Design Manager: Rosamund Saunders
Designer: Ben Ruocco
Photographer: Philip Wilkins

British Library Cataloguing in Publication Data
Oxlade, Chris
   Joining materials. - (Working with materials)
   1.Manufacturing processes - Juvenile literature
   I.Title
   670

ISBN-10: 0-7502-4904-8
ISBN-13: 978-0-7502-4904-1

Cover photograph: a carpenter joins wood together using
a mitre joint.

Photo credits: Lester Lefkowitz/Getty Images title page and 14;
Saed Hindash/Corbis 6; Dorling Kindersley 7; Davies & Starr/Getty
Images 8; Lester Lefkowitz/Getty Images 9; Dorling Kindersley 10;
Emil Pozar/Alamy 11; David R. Frazier Photolibrary, Inc/Alamy 12;
Phil Degginger/Alamy 12; Luis Castaneda Inc/Getty Images 15;
Phil Degginger/Getty Images 16; Jiri Rezac/Alamy 17;
Andy Bullock/Getty Images 17; Laurence Dutton/Getty Images 19;
Jim Craigmyle/Corbis 20; Jacqui Hurst/Corbis 21; Charles
Gupton/Corbis 22; Dorling Kindersley 23; Arthur Tilley/Getty
Images 24; Laura Dwight/Corbis 25; Philip Wilkins 26-27.

The publishers would like to thank models Philippa and Sophie
Campbell for appearing in the photographs.

CONTENTS

Words in **bold** can be found in the glossary on page 28

Joining materials

Everything around you is made up of materials. Everyday materials include paper, plastic, metal and glass. We use these materials to make objects, such as this book or your clothes.

← *Glueing is just one of the ways we join together pieces of material.*

Glue, screws, nuts and bolts, nails and zips are all things we use to join materials. We use them to make joints between pieces of material. The way we make a joint depends on the materials we want to join.

↑ *This person is joining two pieces of wood with a screw.*

7

Nuts, bolts and screws

Two pieces of material, such as wood and metal, can be joined with nuts and bolts or screws. The bolt is put through a hole in a material and the nut is put on the end of the bolt. Then the nut is turned. This pulls the two pieces of material tightly together.

↓ *There is a long groove around the outside of the bolt and another on the inside of the nut. The two grooves fit into each other.*

↑ *This worker is doing up giant nuts and bolts that hold together the metal frame of a building.*

A screw has a sharp, pointed end and a groove around the outside. When a screw is turned the groove cuts into the material. This makes the screw dig slowly into the material.

Sticking together

Objects, such as plastic toys, can be joined with glue. First, the glue is spread on the surfaces of both pieces of material. Then the pieces are pressed together firmly. When the glue dries the pieces are stuck together.

← *Wallpaper paste is made by mixing powder with water. It glues wallpaper firmly to a wall.*

← *Special glue for plastic is needed to join the parts of a plastic model kit.*

It's a Fact!

Some glues come from plants and animals. For example, a glue called gum is made from the sticky liquid from gum trees.

The glue we use for a job depends on the materials we want to join, and on how strongly we want to join them together. For example, we can use **waterproof** glue for some jobs, such as glueing shower tiles to the wall.

Super-strong glues

Sometimes we need to glue materials together very strongly. To do this we can use super-strong glues. Some super-strong glues come in two parts. The parts must be mixed together to make the glue go hard.

↓ *This workman is glueing down floorboards in a new house. He is using special wood glue.*

12

↑ *Plywood is made by joining thin sheets of wood with strong glue. It is used for making floors and walls.*

Strong glues are used to make materials called laminates. A laminate is made by glueing sheets of material together. Cardboard and **plywood** are **laminate** materials.

It's a Fact!

Aircraft wings are made by glueing materials such as metal and plastic together. This makes the wings light and strong.

13

Welding metal

Welding is a way of joining together two pieces of metal. The joint is called a weld. Both pieces of material are heated until they melt. More **molten** metal is added to the joint so it flows into the gap and cools. This leaves a strong joint.

← *The shipyard welder is joining metal. A big spark made by electricity melts the metal.*

14

↑ *The robot welds the metal parts of a car together.*

Many industries use welding to make objects from pieces of metal. Objects from giant cruise ships to mountain bikes are welded together. Metal beams in buildings and bridges are often welded together, too.

It's a Fact!

Some plastics can be welded. For example, the edges of plastic shopping bags are welded together.

15

Soldering metal

Soldering is another way of joining pieces of metal together. A special material called solder is heated up until it melts. It flows between the pieces of metal. It quickly cools and joins the metals together.

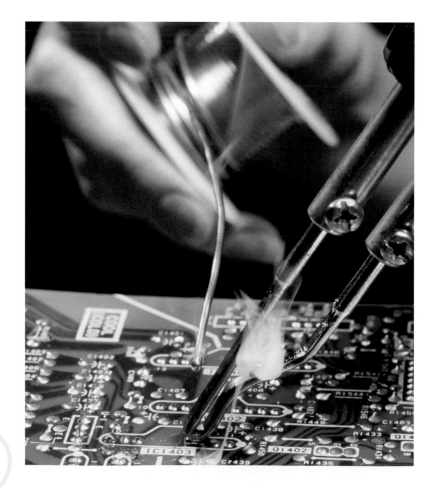

← A tool called a **soldering iron** is used to heat up the metals.

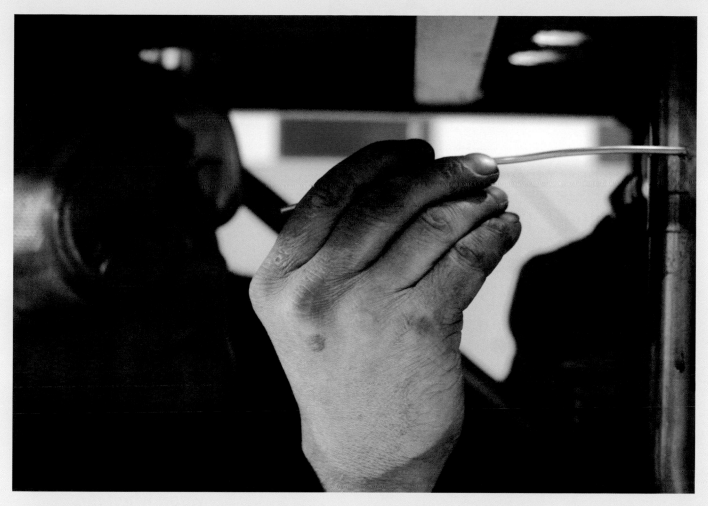

↑ *This plumber is heating the ends of a pipe with a hot flame, ready to add solder to the joint.*

Soldering is used to join wires and other parts together. The solder joins the parts and also lets electricity flow between them. Plumbers join metal water pipes with solder. The solder makes a waterproof joint.

It's a Fact!

The solder used in electronics contains the metals tin and lead. This makes it melt easily.

17

Joining wood

We make all sorts of things from wood, including toys, ornaments, tables, chairs, cupboards and some houses. We join pieces of wood together with nails, screws, nuts and bolts, and glue.

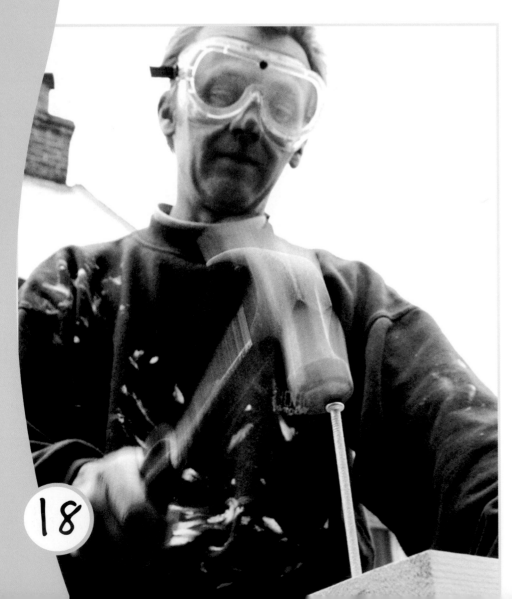

← A nail is a long, thin piece of metal with a sharpened end. It grips the wood when it is hammered in.

↑ *Flat-pack furniture* comes with the screws, nuts and bolts needed to put the parts together.

The method we use to join pieces of wood often depends on how neat the joint must look. Nails are used for fences and sheds. But glue and screws are used for good quality furniture because they give a neat finish.

Wood joints

Carpenters are craftsmen who work with wood. Carpenters normally use special joints between pieces of wood. They cut away wood on each piece so that the pieces lock together. This makes a strong, neat joint.

← This carpenter is making a drawer. The joint he is using is called a dovetail joint.

↑ *This picture frame has a joint at each corner. The joint used is called a mitre joint.*

Some wood joints slot together. The end of one piece of wood slots tightly into a hole in the other piece of wood. This makes a strong joint.

It's a Fact!

Hundreds of years ago carpenters built huge ships from wood using joints like mitre and dovetail joints.

21

Joining soft materials

Some materials, such as fabrics and paper, are soft and bendy. We use glue, metal staples and thread to join soft materials together. We also use sticky tape. Tape is made up of a plastic strip with a layer of glue on one side.

← *This girl is using sticky tape to join pieces of wrapping paper together.*

↑ *Thread is used to stitch two
pieces of fabric together.*

We join pieces of fabric together with
thread. The thread passes backwards
and forwards through the layers of
fabric. This makes a line of stitches.

It's a Fact!

Stitching can make
a very strong joint.
Safety **harnesses**
and **parachutes**
are held together
by strong stitching.

Temporary joints

We often need to join two pieces of material for a short time so we can take them apart again. This is called a **temporary** joint. For example, sticky note pads are designed to stick to a desk and then be peeled off again.

↓ *The glue on a sticking plaster makes a temporary joint. The plaster can be pulled off again.*

↑ *These bats are covered with tiny hooks. They make a temporary joint with the furry ball.*

Many clothes have temporary joints. The joints allow you to take clothes on and off easily. For example, a coat has a zip down the front that joins the two sides together. Buttons can be used to join fabrics temporarily.

It's a Fact!

The **hook-and-loop fastener** was invented in 1948 by George de Mestral. He got the idea on a walk, when plant seeds covered in tiny hooks got stuck to his trousers.

25

Activities

Flour and water glue

Make your own glue using everyday materials.

What you need		
plain flour	spoon	salt
water	bowl	sieve
cup	airtight container	

① Pour about a quarter of a cup of plain flour into a bowl.

② Fill the cup with water. Slowly add the water to the flour. Keep mixing so that you don't get any lumps. Sieve the glue if there are some lumps.

③ Add a few pinches of salt to the glue. This will stop mould growing in it. You have made flour and water glue.

④ You can make the glue thicker by boiling it in a pan for a few minutes. Ask an adult to do this for you. Let the glue cool before you touch it.

⑤ Store the glue in an **airtight** container. You can use the glue to stick paper together.

Papier mâché head

Use your flour and water glue to join newspaper to a balloon.

What you need

newspaper	large paintbrush
flour-and-water glue or	balloon
made-up wallpaper paste	

① Tear plenty of strips of paper about 3 cm wide.

② Blow up a balloon and tie its neck.

③ Brush glue onto both sides of a strip of paper and stick it onto the balloon.

④ Add more strips until the balloon is covered with paper strips.

⑤ Let the paper dry.

⑥ Repeat this process two more times.

⑦ Prick the balloon to burst it.
The material you have made is called papier mâché. It is like a laminate material, built up of layers of paper and glue. The papier mâché head is now ready to decorate.

Glossary

airtight stops air getting in or out

flat-pack furniture furniture that you buy in pieces and put together at home

harness a set of straps that fits around a person's body and is used to attach the person to a rope

hook-and-loop fastener a tiny hook that catches on a tiny loop to hold material together

laminate a material made by glueing together thin sheets of material

molten heated up until melted

parachute a large piece of fabric that lets a skydiver fall slowly to the ground

plywood a material made by glueing thin sheets of wood on top of each other

soldering iron a tool used to heat up solder to make joints

temporary when something is designed not to last forever

waterproof does not let water get through

Further information

BOOKS

How We Use: Metals/Paper/Rubber/Wood
by Chris Oxlade, Raintree (2005)

A Material World: It's Glass/It's Metal/It's Plastic/It's Wood
by Kay Davies and Wendy Oldfield, Wayland (2006)

Investigating Science: How do we use materials?
by Jacqui Bailey, Franklin Watts (2005)

WEBSITES

doityourself.com/wood/h2woodjoints.htm
Pictures of all the different ways of joining wood

www.diydoctor.org.uk/projects/typesofnail.htm
Which nails are used for different jobs

PLACES TO VISIT

Eureka, Halifax
www.eureka.org.uk

Glasgow Science Centre
www.glasgowsciencecentre.org

The Science Museum, London
www.sciencemuseum.org.uk

Index

All the numbers in **bold** refer to photographs.